Style Secrets

SKIN
CARE
&
MAKEUP
TIPS & TRICKS

KAREN LATCHANA KENNEY

ILLUSTRATED BY ELENA HESCHKE

Lerner Publications ◆ Minneapolis

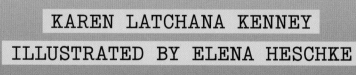

Lerner Publications Company
A division of Lerner Publishing Group, Inc.
241 First Avenue North
Minneapolis, MN 55401 USA

For reading levels and more information, look up this title at
www.lernerbooks.com.

Main body text set in Grotesque MT Std. Light 10/14.
Typeface provided by Monotype.

Library of Congress Cataloging-in-Publication Data

Kenney, Karen Latchana.
    Skin care & makeup tips & tricks / by Karen Latchana Kenney ; illustrated by
Elena Heschke.
        pages   cm. — (Style secrets)
    Includes index.
    ISBN 978-1-4677-5219-0 (lib. bdg. : alk. paper)
    ISBN 978-1-4677-8656-0 (EB pdf)
    1. Skin—Care and hygiene—Juvenile literature. 2. Cosmetics—Juvenile
literature. 3. Beauty, Personal—Juvenile literature. I. Heschke, Elena, illustrator.
II. Title. III. Title: Skin care and makeup tips and tricks.
RL87.K48 2016
616.5—dc23   2014024892

Manufactured in the United States of America
1 – VP – 7/15/15

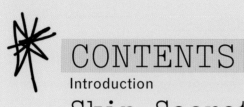

CONTENTS

Introduction

SKIN SECRETS

Let's face it—your skin is a big deal! It covers your entire body. No wonder you spend so much time taking care of it—especially the skin on your face. And no wonder a huge pimple can make for a bad day.

So how can you keep your skin looking its very best? Start with good skin care. That includes everything from nutrition to cleansing, toning, exfoliating, and moisturizing. Special treatments help out with problem areas. And it's a constant game of adjustments—your skin changes every day.

Makeup can be fun, but it only looks as good as its base—your skin. With great skin, you don't *need* a lot of makeup. But little touches here and there can enhance your natural beauty and reflect your unique style.

Some simple tips and tricks can be your starting point for making your skin feel and look top-notch. Not every product or method will work for you, but once you know the basics, you can figure out what *does* work. Then you can get creative with your look. You can make your skin and makeup healthy, fresh, fun, and *all* you.

Chapter 1

HEALTHY SKIN

Healthy skin simply glows. It feels soft and looks smooth. And it also reacts to things it doesn't like—from harsh, cold winter winds to a lack of water or sleep.

To care for your skin properly, begin by thinking about how you care for your body as a whole. Do you eat healthy, fresh foods? Do you drink enough water? Do you get enough sleep? Poor nutrition and other bad habits will show up on your skin.

Outside factors also damage skin. You need protection against changing weather. Extra moisturizer helps in dry weather. And sunscreen is essential when you're outside—even when it's cloudy or cold!

The next step to making skin happy is getting to know it well. Look at your face in a mirror from about half an arm's length away. Can you see pores in your skin? That's fine. *Where* do you see pores? On your cheeks? Your chin? The sides of your face?

If you have visible pores in all these places and your skin tends to get shiny during the day, you probably have an oily skin type. Your skin makes too much oil, which can lead to large pores, acne, and shine.

Are your visible pores mostly just in the center of your face? You probably have a normal skin type. You're lucky—your skin naturally produces the right amount of oil and moisture. It won't give you much trouble if you treat it well.

What if you barely see any pores? That means you likely have a dry skin type. Dry skin doesn't produce enough moisture. It can feel rough and look dull.

Of course, not everyone has just one skin type. Some people have combination skin, with different types in different areas of the face. And don't forget that weather, stress, and even diet can affect how your skin looks. For instance, a really harsh winter might dry out your skin even if you have an oily skin type. And if you're not getting enough sleep, you may have breakouts even if your skin type is normal. But once you've pegged your skin type—or types—you'll have an easier time figuring out how to give it the care it needs.

Foods to Make You Glow

Some foods contain vitamins, acids, and minerals that keep your skin healthy and glowing. Here are a few to try:

- **Yogurt, milk, and other dairy products.** These foods are rich in vitamin A, which keeps cell reproduction under control. (Overproducing skin cells can lead to clogged pores.) A serving of yogurt each day can put you on the path to clearer, smoother skin.

- **Blackberries, blueberries, strawberries, and plums.** Get a big dose of antioxidants by eating these fruits. Antioxidants help protect skin from sun damage.

- **Salmon, walnuts, and flaxseeds.** The fatty acids in these foods strengthen skin cell walls. Strong cell walls keep more water in your skin. This makes your skin soft and smooth. So try snacking on a few flaxseed crackers or a handful of walnuts each day.

BASIC CARE

Every day, both morning and night, follow a few simple steps to keep your skin clean. Never go to bed without cleaning your face, whether or not you've worn makeup that day. Some basic skin care products will make this process easy. You can find the products you need at many retail stores or online.

Makeup remover. Some makeup is washable. You can remove it just by scrubbing thoroughly with warm water. But nonwashable products are more common. If you opt for these, you'll need to invest in makeup remover. Use makeup remover wipes on your face. For your eyes, get eye makeup remover solution or pads. Wipe these around your eyes to remove mascara, eye shadow, and liner. Not keen on all that paper waste? A small amount of coconut oil will do the job too. Just rub it on your face or around your eyes with your fingers and then rinse it off.

Cleanser. Cleansing removes dirt, oil, and stubborn leftover makeup from your face. Many cleansers are gels that turn to foam when you add a little water. You gently rub this foam on just-washed, already-damp skin. Then rinse it off. Use a cleanser that's targeted at your skin type.

Toner. Sometimes using cleanser isn't enough to tame breakouts—especially during hot weather or for really oily skin. So you may want to add a toner to your skin care routine. Toners are usually lotions or liquids that you apply to your face after cleansing. Some toners help keep oiliness under control. Others hydrate dry skin.

Moisturizer. Before you go out for the day, be sure to moisturize! Moisturizer protects your skin from cold winds or other harsh weather. It also makes a smooth base for makeup. If you have an oily skin type, look for oil-free moisturizer. Many moisturizers contain an SPF (sun protection factor). This helps shield your skin from harmful sun rays.

LAVENDER TONER

Try this toner for acne-prone skin. Witch hazel is a natural astringent that keeps skin from getting too oily. You can find it at many retail stores. Lavender oil heals and soothes damaged skin. Look for essential oils at health food stores or online.

What You Need:

- witch hazel
- lavender essential oil
- a 1-ounce (28-gram) spray bottle

Here's How:

1. Fill the spray bottle with witch hazel, leaving a little room at the top.

2. Add 10 drops of lavender oil.

3. Put the cap back on the bottle. Shake to mix.

4. Cleanse your face as usual.

5. Spritz the spray bottle's contents on your face.

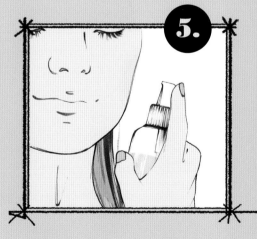

Stay Safe from the Sun!

Sun exposure can cause serious skin damage, including brown spots and even skin cancer. If your moisturizer doesn't have an SPF, apply a sunscreen about fifteen minutes before you go outside. (And if you're spending most of the day outdoors, reapply it every couple of hours.)

SPECIAL TREATMENTS

Sometimes your skin needs a little extra care. Maybe you're having a major breakout. Or your skin may just look a bit blah. Special treatments can help out in a big way. You only need to use them once a week or once a month (depending on the instructions and your skin's needs). They can be just what you need to fix those problem areas.

Masks. Some masks hydrate, leaving your skin dewy and soft. Clay or peel-off masks extract oils and impurities, which is especially good for acne-prone skin. Exfoliating masks brighten dull skin. They remove the surface layer of dead skin cells and expose the bright, fresh skin below. Most masks need to be applied to clean skin and left on for five to fifteen minutes before being washed off. Follow the directions on the label, and make sure to pick a mask that targets your skin's needs.

Scrubs. These gels and lotions contain small scrubbing beads or grains. They buff away dry or dead skin, revealing the new skin below. This gives your skin a healthy glow. Massage a scrub onto your skin for a few minutes and then wash it off. Gentle scrubs can be used every day. Deep-cleaning scrubs should be used only once or twice a week. Scrubs are also very easy to make at home. One very simple scrub contains two parts brown sugar and one part olive oil.

Spot treatments. Need some help with a small problem area? Acne gels or creams work to dry up pimples and help skin heal. Intense moisturizers can help severely dry skin. These kinds of treatments should only be used as needed. If your products aren't doing the trick, consult a doctor for advice. Doctors can prescribe treatments not found in stores.

Eco-Friendly Face Care

Many skin care products, especially scrubs, contain microbeads. These tiny plastic balls are great for scrubbing away dead skin cells but not so great for the environment. After they go down your sink drain, they often end up in lakes and rivers. You can help the environment by paying a little extra for facial scrubs that don't use microbeads. Or you can make your own natural scrub!

OATMEAL SODA SCRUB

This super-simple scrub gently buffs away dead skin. The oatmeal's grains are a natural exfoliant. Oatmeal and baking soda also absorb oil and dirt.

What You Need:

- measuring spoons
- 2 tablespoons oatmeal
- 1 teaspoon baking soda
- a bowl
- water
- a spoon
- a basin

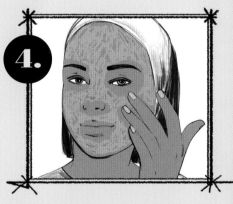

Here's How:

1. Mix oatmeal and baking soda in a bowl.

2. Add enough water to make a sticky paste. Stir well.

3. Wash your face and leave your skin slightly damp.

4. Gently massage the paste onto your face for a few minutes.

5. Rinse off the paste over the basin. (The oatmeal may clog a sink's drain.) Empty the basin down a kitchen sink garbage disposal, or pour the water into the sink through a strainer and then empty the oatmeal into the trash.

6. Pat your skin dry and then tone and moisturize.

Stop! Don't Pop!

It can be hard to resist popping a pimple. But popping often leads to bigger problems. Bacteria can spread into other pores, creating even more pimples. And popped pimples can lead to permanent scars. So cover your problem areas with concealer during the day, use a spot treatment before bed, and the rest of the time, avoid touching those areas!

Chapter 2

SCENT AND STYLE

Have you smelled yourself lately? You should—it says a lot about you. A scent is just as personal as your skin type or your makeup. You want it to reflect who you are—and not distract from the rest of you.

The first step to smelling good is showering regularly. Sweat and bacteria create body odor, and that can be bad news. Wear clean clothes and use deodorant to keep body odor from taking control.

SIMPLE DEODORANT

You can make some all-natural deodorant with just a few ingredients. For this basic recipe, pick up a jar of coconut oil for a few dollars at a grocery store or order some online.

What You Need:

- measuring spoons
- 4 tablespoons baking soda
- 4 tablespoons cornstarch
- 6 tablespoons coconut oil
- essential oil in a scent of your choice (optional)
- a bowl
- a spoon
- a small, empty plastic container with a lid

Here's How:

1. Mix baking soda, cornstarch, and coconut oil together in the bowl.

2. If you wish, add 20 to 25 drops of your favorite essential oil—or a few drops apiece of several different oils—for a personalized scent.

3. Pour the mixture into a small container with a lid.

4. Run two fingers over the mixture and apply it to your armpits.

5. Tightly attach the container's lid and get ready to work up a sweat!

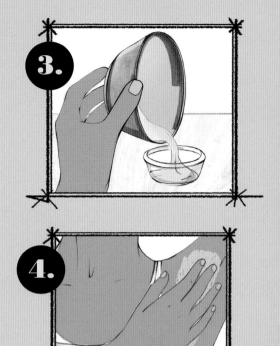

Investing in Essential Oils

A bottle of essential oil lasts for years. You only need 10 to 20 drops to make a scent. Some bottles cost as little as a few dollars apiece. Find them at natural foods stores and from online retailers. To create a distinctive scent, try one of these combinations or make up your own!

- Lavender Musk: 10 drops cedarwood and 10 drops lavender, plus a splash of pure vanilla extract

- Citrus Cedar: 10 drops cedarwood, 10 drops sweet orange

- Floral Freshness: 8 drops lavender, 8 drops rosemary, 2 drops lemon

THE PERFECT PERFUME

You can keep it natural with a just-showered, fresh smell. Or you can add a scent that you love. Perfumes come in a nearly endless range of scents—from woodsy to earthy to floral. You can also use essential oils to make your own perfumes. Just be sure to use a scent sparingly. Too much overpowers a room. Let your scent help *you* shine.

SOLID PERFUME

What's your favorite scent? Make up your own with a solid perfume. It's easy, smells great, and is portable too. You can find the beeswax beads you'll need at a co-op, a natural foods store, a craft store, or online. Before you start working, get an adult's OK to use a stove for a few minutes.

What You Need:

- measuring spoons
- 1 cup water
- $1\frac{1}{2}$ tablespoons beeswax beads
- $1\frac{1}{2}$ tablespoons sweet almond oil or olive oil
- 20 drops essential oil of your choice
- a glass measuring cup
- a small saucepan
- a small bowl
- an oven mitt
- a spoon
- a small container with a lid, such as an old, cleaned eye shadow container

Here's How:

1. Boil the water in the saucepan over medium heat.

2. Measure the beeswax beads into the measuring cup. Set the measuring cup in the boiling water.

3. Let the beeswax beads melt. It may take 5 to 7 minutes. Meanwhile, work on step 4.

4. Add the almond or olive oil to the small bowl. Mix in the essential oil. Use one type of essential oil or try a combination.

5. When the beads are melted, turn off the burner. Use the oven mitt to carefully remove the measuring cup from the saucepan. The measuring cup will be hot.

6. Place the measuring cup on a heatproof surface. Quickly stir in the oil mixture, before the wax starts to harden.

7. Pour the hot wax perfume into the small container. Let it sit and harden for about 30 minutes.

8. Rub a small amount of solid perfume on your wrists. As your skin warms the wax, your scent is released.

Chapter 3
MAKEUP TOOLS

You've laid the groundwork for healthy skin that looks and even smells its best. So you're ready to explore the world of makeup. And there's no shortage of products to choose from. Foundation, eyeliner, mascara, lip gloss, concealer . . . the possibilities are nearly endless. Where do you start?

BASICS AND BEYOND

The first step on a successful makeup journey is to gather the right tools. You'll need these tools to blend, smooth, and evenly distribute makeup on your face. Choosing them well and taking care of them will help turn you into a true makeup artist.

Brushes. Makeup is only as good as the brush you use to apply it. A contouring brush is perfect for blush. Apply liquid foundation with a fluid brush. An eyeliner brush makes defined lines, while a crease brush is designed for eyelids. Natural bristles made from animal hair work well for dry makeup. Synthetic bristles are good for wet makeup.

Sponges and puffs. You might use sponges to apply cream or liquid makeup. They help blend makeup smoothly on the face. Most are disposable, but you can reuse them if you wash and air-dry them between makeup applications. Powder puffs help you pat on powdered makeup for even coverage. Wash them weekly in soapy water.

Eye extras. Eyelash curlers make your eyelashes pop. (Use them before, not after, you apply mascara. Mascara can make eyelashes brittle. They may break when curled.) Eyelash combs also come in handy. They separate stuck-together lashes and remove unsightly mascara clumps.

Brow backup. Tweezers keep your eyebrows from becoming too unruly. When you're shopping for tweezers, look at the tips. Are they slanted, square, or pointed? Slanted tips are generally best for eyebrows. To cut long brows, you can also use mini scissors. Comb your eyebrow hair upward with a brow brush and cut off extra-long strands to keep your brows looking tidy.

BRUSH SOAP

Use this deep-cleaning yet gentle soap to take the grime off your makeup brushes. Cleaning just once a month keeps brushes looking and working like new.

What You Need:

- measuring spoons
- 1 tablespoon dish soap
- 1 tablespoon white vinegar
- 1 cup warm water
- a tall cup or glass
- dirty makeup brushes

Here's How:

1. Pour the water, the dish soap, and the vinegar into the glass. Mix until the soap dissolves into the water.

2. Put your brushes into the mixture, bristle side down. Let them soak for a few minutes.

3. Lift up the brushes, gently shake them in the glass, and take them all the way out.

4. Rinse the bristles with warm water and then cold water.

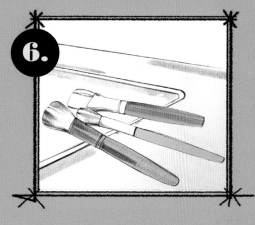

5. Shake out the water and straighten the bristles with your fingers.

6. Lay the brushes at the end of a sink, with the bristles extending over the edge, to air-dry them.

Be Good to Your Brushes

Always store brushes upright, with the bristles up. This helps keep them clean. Wash brushes regularly with a cleaning solution. Dirty brushes won't work as well. They can also spread germs and bacteria onto your face, resulting in pimples. Rinse brushes with soap and water every few days, and give them a longer soak in a cleaning solution once a month.

MAKEUP CARE

Once you have the tools you want, you can start stocking up on the real deal: makeup products themselves. How do you know what products will work well for you? Trial and error. Buy a little makeup at a time, in small containers, until you've figured out what you—and your skin—like.

Finding the right makeup and supplies can take a while. It's also a big investment. Get the most out of your products by making sure you don't waste or lose them.

First and foremost, use a makeup organizer to store your makeup. Find a container with different compartments. Or make your own by recycling cups or boxes. An organizer makes it easy to keep different types of makeup in separated areas. Knowing what you have will save you from buying doubles.

Store your makeup in a cool, dry place. Extreme temperatures may cause makeup to quickly go bad. Make sure caps are tightly closed, and clean up any spills or leaks right away.

Even if you're taking good care of your products, makeup doesn't last forever. Eventually many products dry out. And even before that happens, makeup can start to collect harmful bacteria. So check your makeup's packaging. Some products list expiration dates and storage directions. Pay attention to these suggestions. Makeup used past its prime can cause skin and eye problems.

Be especially careful with eye makeup. Eyeliner, mascara, and eye shadow don't last as long as other types of makeup. They can easily spread bacteria to your eyes and cause infections. And never add water or saliva to dried-out mascara. This makes it easier for bacteria to grow.

Short makeup shelf life is another reason to buy makeup in small quantities when you can. You don't want to end up with ten different shades of eye shadow that have gone bad. Build your collection a little at a time. Notice how much of a product you use each day or each week—and how long it takes for something to run out. Then, when you know you're a day or two away from finishing a product, you can buy a replacement.

Makeup Shelf Life

It's tempting to hang on to makeup until you've used every last drop. But make sure you use it before it becomes a playground for bacteria. Here's how long most makeup products last:

- Liquid foundation—6 to 12 months

- Liquid concealer—1 year

- Powder and stick concealer—2 years

- Face powder—2 years

- Powder blush—2 years

- Cream blush—1 year

- Powder eye shadow—3 months

- Liquid or pencil eyeliner—3 months

- Mascara—3 months

- Lipsticks and glosses—1 year

Chapter 4

MAKEUP IN ACTION

The way you apply your makeup is just as important as the products you use. So as you experiment with the products you've bought, think carefully about your techniques. More makeup does not equal a better look. You just need a little, applied with the right tools and in the right ways. From your skin to your eyes and cheeks, makeup should enhance, not hide, your natural and unique beauty.

FACE-FIRST

Skin doesn't always look even. It might be a bit blotchy. You might have a few pimples or dark circles under your eyes. That's where foundation comes in. It gives you an even base for the rest of your makeup—or just a smooth finish that you can leave as is. You can find both liquid and powder foundation. Pick a color that closely matches your skin tone.

It's easy to go heavy on foundation, but that's something you want to avoid. If it's too thick, it can look like a mask. And foundation can clog pores, causing breakouts. Let your skin shine through. A circle of liquid foundation about the size of a nickel can work for your entire face. Dab dots of that small portion onto the main areas that need coverage—for instance, your forehead, cheeks, and chin. Blend it in well and set it with some powder. And don't forget to remove makeup before you go to bed.

A tinted moisturizer is an alternative to regular foundation. This has lighter coverage and gives a much more natural look. It's also less likely to clog pores.

If you have sensitive skin, some of the chemicals in foundation can worsen your skin problems. You may want to invest in mineral makeup. It tends to be pricier than regular foundation, but it leaves out many ingredients that can irritate skin. It's also oil-free. That's good news if you have naturally oily skin.

Want to cover up pimples or dark spots? Pat on some liquid concealer, let it dry, and set it with some loose powder. Liquid concealer works well for all skin types, including oily skin. If you have dry or normal skin, you might try a cream or stick concealer. Stick concealers are solid, like lipstick. They're not ideal for oily skin because they can clog pores.

Concealer can disguise a problem spot, but it won't make it disappear. Remember, the best skin is healthy skin. Focus on your basic skin care. You'll have fewer flaws to hide and need to use less makeup.

Read the Label!

If you have sensitive or oily skin, look for "hypoallergenic" or "noncomedogenic" makeup. *Hypoallergenic* means that a product is less likely to cause allergic reactions. *Noncomedogenic* means that the ingredients shouldn't block or clog pores.

EYE OF THE MAKEUP HOLDER

You can do a lot to play with your eyes. Make them dramatic for a night out on the weekend. Or create a softer look for everyday wear. Here are some eye basics you might want to add to your makeup collection:

<u>Eye shadow.</u> Eye shadow comes in powder and cream forms. It also comes in many styles and colors. Matte has a dull finish, while a shimmer has sheer color and some sparkle. Satin shadow has a less dramatic sparkle. Frosted shadow has a white or silver sparkle and often comes in pastel colors. Natural makeup colors—like soft pinks, grays, peaches, browns, and coppers—are earthy and subtle. Some colors enhance your eye color too. If you have a light eye color, you need less color on your lids. Try gray browns, gold, or slate gray for blue eyes. For brown eyes, try bronze or peach shadows. Green eyes really pop with mauves and rosy golds. Hazel eyes love hints of gold in mushroom, khaki, or golden-gray shadows.

<u>Eyeliner.</u> Use eyeliner to define your eyes along your lash line. Liquid eyeliner makes a very precise line. Soft eyeliner looks more natural. Where you apply liner is important too. For close-set eyes, start your line near the middle of the eyes. This helps emphasize the space between your eyes. Wider-set or larger eyes can be lined all the way from the inner to the outer corners. Black eyeliner may be harsh for fair skin but stands out well on darker skin. Browns and grays are other options.

<u>Mascara.</u> A flourish of mascara can add the finishing touch to your look. Waterproof mascara won't run down your face if you get caught in the rain—or caught up in a tearjerker movie or book. That makes it tough to remove, though. Some eye makeup remover is geared specifically for waterproof mascara. But some olive oil or baby oil on a cotton ball or a cotton swab will work too.

NATURAL EYES

Just a little shadow, liner, and mascara can create a look that's perfect for daytime adventures, including school.

What You Need:
- eye shadow
- eyeliner in a brown or gray color
- an eyelash curler
- mascara

Here's How:

1. Brush eye shadow along the lash line of your upper eyelid.

2. Blend shadow up to your crease or the middle of your eyelid. Make sure shadow has a blended, soft edge.

3. Dot eyeliner between top lashes. This makes a soft line that defines your eyes.

4. Curl eyelashes. Then sweep some mascara lightly over lashes.

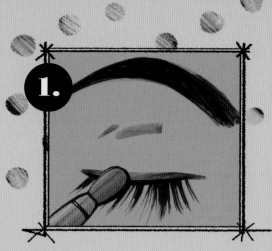

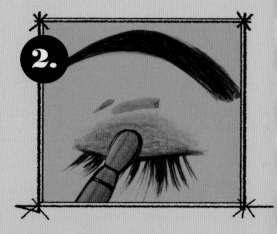

CLEAN BROWS

Unruly eyebrows can take over your face if you let them. They need to be shaped and maintained. Clean brows help your eyes stand out.

Most eyebrow overhauls are done in one of two ways: tweezing or waxing. Tweezing is easy to do at home. All you need is a pair of tweezers and some spare time. Use the tweezers to pluck each hair out individually. Tweezing should be done every few days, depending on your hair color and type. People with light, thin hair can get away without tweezing for longer than those with darker or thicker hair.

Waxing uses warm wax and cloth waxing strips. The wax lifts out multiple hairs at a time. You can buy at-home waxing kits or even make your own waxing solution. If you use a kit, follow the directions carefully. You don't want to accidentally take off half an eyebrow! And if you have sensitive skin, waxing may cause irritation.

If eyebrows get a little too thin in spots, you can fill in your brows with some brow liner or matching eye shadow. Don't go too dark, or your brows could look harsh. Follow where your brows naturally go. They'll be cleaned up but still exactly right for you.

Eyebrow Shapes

Eyebrows come in all varieties: thin and thick, light and dark, dramatically arched and nearly straight. Finding the right eyebrow shape for your face is easy—because you already have it. You can thicken brows with makeup or thin them out with beauty tools, but always let them stay true to their natural, unique shape.

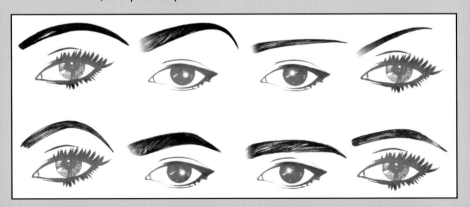

FIND YOUR ARCH

Stick to your natural arch when cleaning up your brows. Start by removing stray hairs from along the bottom of your brows. (Plucking hairs along the top edge of your brows can distort your brows' natural shape.) Follow these easy steps to find your arch:

What You Need:

- a mirror
- a pencil

Here's How:

1. Measure from the side of your nose by your nostril. Place a pencil alongside your nostril, pointing straight up to the inner tip of your eye. Where it hits your brow is where your brow should begin. You can trim any hairs that extend past this point, closer to the center of your face.

2. Lay the pencil at a 45-degree angle from your nose and over your eyelid. It should line up with your iris if you open your eye. Where it hits your eyebrow is the highest point of its arch. If hairs elsewhere along your brow extend higher than this point, trim them.

3. Lay the pencil from the edge of your nostril to the outer corner of your eye. Where it hits the brow is where your brow should end. Trim hairs that extend beyond this point.

TIPS FOR LIPS

What about your lips? They can be shiny, sparkly, pale, or bright. Balance the color with the rest of your makeup. If you have darker eye makeup, go for a pale, nude lip. But if you have minimal makeup, a bright tone can look good. And if you need to remove your lip color, just use a cotton ball soaked with baby oil to wipe your lips clean. Then rinse with water.

Lip balm. Tinted lip balms are the way to go if you just want a hint of color and an easy application. The bonus? Lip balms provide tons of moisture to dry lips. Many also have an SPF to protect lips from the sun's harmful rays.

Lip gloss. A little gloss makes lips super shiny. It's also a short-term lip color. But watch out! Gloss can be sticky. It tends to catch stray hairs and rub off on glasses. Gloss also usually wears off easily. Carry some with you in a pocket or a bag for easy reapplication.

Lip stain. These last a really long time—from eight to twelve hours. They tint your lips without thickly coating them. Take your time to apply a lip stain perfectly. Stains are a bit harder to remove than other lip products. You'll need to use makeup remover to erase the color.

Lipstick. To add some real pizazz to your lips, try a little lipstick. It comes in different finishes: matte, satin, gloss, glaze, and luster. Each has its own degree of shine or sparkle. Just reapply lipstick often to make your color last. And check your teeth! Lipstick tends to rub off easily.

SWEET LIP SCRUB

Soft, smooth lips can be hard to come by in dry climates or during harsh winters. Use this simple, sweet scrub once a week. It'll help prevent cracks and flakiness, allowing gloss and lipstick to glide on.

What You Need:

- 1 tablespoon sugar
- ½ teaspoon olive oil
- ½ teaspoon honey
- a small bowl
- a spoon
- a damp paper towel or cloth

Here's How:

1. Mix the sugar, the oil, and the honey in the small bowl.

2. Rub about a teaspoon of the scrub on your lips. Massage it in for about 1 minute.

3. Gently wipe off the mixture with a damp paper towel or cloth.

Cool for School?

It's fun to wear some wild makeup for a party. But at school, make sure your makeup is appropriate. Go easy on foundation, eye makeup, and lip color. (After all, who wants to get up extra early on a school day to put on a ton of makeup?) Keep your eyebrows plucked and clean, but not so thin that they look unnatural.

HEALTHY GLOW

Hoping to add some extra glow or shimmer to your cheeks? Blush is your friend. Pick from powder, cream, or tints. Powder blush needs to be applied with a brush. It gives you the most color, but it sits on top of your skin. This can highlight blemishes. Cream blush sinks into the skin a bit more, creating a dewy glow. Apply it with your fingers. And liquid blush and cheek stains are sheer, creating a lighter color. Use fingers or a synthetic brush to apply.

Most blush comes in either matte or shimmery colors. Matte gives a more natural look. Shimmer adds sparkle but doesn't look very natural. Use it for special occasions or to help define your features at night. And keep other makeup minimal with shimmery cheeks.

Not all blush works well on all skin colors. Light pinks get lost on dark skin. And deep plum looks harsh on fair skin. For fair skin, try light pinks, peaches, and corals. For medium skin tones, use deeper corals or mauves. Dark skin is perfect for deeper hues, like reds and oranges.

ROSY CHEEKS

You need a light touch when applying blush. Too much in the wrong spot can look really bad. Use these steps to get perfect rosy cheeks!

What You Need:
- a powdered blush
- a plush brush
- a mirror

Here's How:

1. Run your brush gently over the blush to get a light coating on the tips of the bristles.

2. Find the area on your face that spans from right in front of your ear to the middle of the cheek.

3. Lightly sweep blush onto the area in an oval shape.

4. Focus blush on the upper cheekbone, not the apple of your cheeks. Blend well.

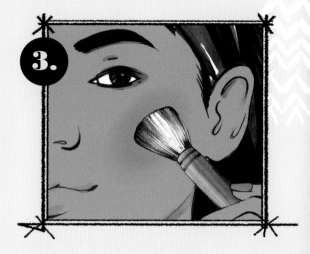

The Real Secret

Great skin doesn't happen overnight. But with the right care, you'll be well on your way to that healthy glow. Don't get discouraged if your skin's giving you trouble. Be patient, practice good habits, and find products geared toward your skin's needs. You'll soon see the difference it all makes! Then makeup can provide the finishing touches.

Have fun doing makeovers on yourself and your friends. Get inspiration online, in fashion magazines, or just by checking out your friends' looks. Focus on one feature at a time, whether it's your eyes, lips, or cheekbones. Before long, you'll have an overall look that lets your natural beauty shine!

GLOSSARY

acne: an inflammation of the skin caused by clogged pores

antioxidant: a substance, such as a vitamin or a mineral, that slows oxidation, a chemical process that can cause cell death

astringent: a substance that cleans skin and minimizes pores

bacteria: tiny organisms that can sometimes cause disease

exfoliant: a substance that removes the surface layer of skin

expiration: the end of the time when something should be used

impurities: unclean substances that can clog pores, such as dirt, oil, and dead skin cells

matte: having a dull surface

pore: a tiny hole in your skin through which sweat is released

synthetic: artificially made instead of found in nature

FURTHER INFORMATION

Brown, Bobbi, and Rebecca Paley. *Beauty Rules: Fabulous Looks, Beauty Essentials, and Life Lessons for Loving Your Teens and Twenties.* San Francisco: Chronicle Books, 2010. Wondering how to make the most of your sometimes frustrating skin? Learn how to bring out your inner beauty here.

Kenney, Karen Latchana. *Hair Care Tips & Tricks*. Minneapolis: Lerner Publications, 2016. Discover more ways to look your best with secrets for healthy hair and fun hairstyles.

Shoket, Ann. *Seventeen Ultimate Guide to Beauty: The Best Hair, Skin, Nails & Makeup Ideas for You.* Philadelphia: Running Press, 2012. Get some more skin care and makeup tricks from the experts.

"Skin Care"—*Teen Vogue*
http://www.teenvogue.com/beauty/skin-care
Get the lowdown on the factors that affect your skin and what you can do to improve its health and looks.

"The Skin You're In: Teaching Guide for Preteens and Young Teens"—American Skin Association
http://www.americanskin.org/education/the_skin_youre_in/pdf/teaching_guide.pdf
Scroll down to the third page of this online activity packet to start testing and expanding your knowledge about skin care.

Willablog
http://willa.com/blog
Get more tips for taking care of your skin—plus instructions for other stylish activities—from tween makeup expert Willa Doss and other young contributors.

INDEX

PHOTO ACKNOWLEDGMENTS

The images in this book are used with the permission of: © Yulia Nikulyasha Nikitina/
Shutterstock, p. 1 (brush); © Simone Andress/Shutterstock, p. 1 (eye shadow);
© Picsfive/Shutterstock, pp. 3, 5 (top), 30; © Eli Maier/Shutterstock, pp. 4 (left),10
(bottom left); © photopixel/Shutterstock, p. 4 (right); © filipw/Shutterstock, pp. 5 (top), 14;
© Konstantin Chagin/Shutterstock, p. 6 (top); © Lucie Lang/Dreamstime, p. 6 (bottom);
© iStockphoto/bluestocking, p. 7; © robert_s/Shutterstock, p. 8; © kubais/Bigstock,
pp. 10 (bottom right), 21 (bottom); © imagehub/Shutterstock, p. 10 (top); © eAlisa/
Shutterstock, p. 12; © Everything/Shutterstock, p. 16 (bottom); © iStockphoto/pederk,
p. 18 (top); © Africa Studio/Shutterstock, pp. 18, 28 (top), 31; © PicsFive/Bigstock,
p. 20 (bottom); © kadroff/Bigstock, p. 21 (top); © mj_23/Bigstock, p. 22 (top left);
© iStockphoto/WEKWEK, p. 22 (top middle, top right); © iStockphoto/imagehub88, p. 22
(bottom left); © iStockphoto/restyler, p. 22 (bottom right); © Antonsov85/Shutterstock,
p. 24 (top); © Julinzy/Shutterstock, p. 24 (bottom); © Artnis/Shutterstock, p. 26; © kedrov/
Shutterstock, p. 28; © iStockphoto/imagehub88, p. 29 (bottom); © Settaphan/Bigstock,
p. 29; © mj_23/Bigstock, p. 32.

Front cover: © Simone Andress/Shutterstock (eye shadow); © Yulia Nikulyasha Nikitina/
Shutterstock (brush).

Back cover: © kedrov/Shutterstock (crushed powder); © kadroff/Bigstock (foundation);
© severija/Shutterstock (glitter).

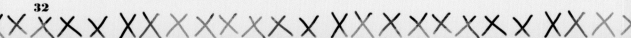